DID YOU HEAR THAT?

By Alfred M. Struthers
Illustrated by Cathy Provoda

No part of this publication may be reprinted or transmitted in any form without written permission of the publisher.
For information regarding permission, write to:

Permissions
Escape Hatch Books
27 Main Street
Jaffrey, NH 03452

permissions@escapehatchbooks.com

ISBN 978-0-9976397-7-3

Copyright 2019 by Alfred M. Struthers
Illustrations copyright 2019 by Cathy Provoda
All rights reserved. Published by Escape Hatch Books
www.escapehatchbooks.com

1 2 3 4 5 6 7 8 9

Printed in the U.S.A.

For
Madelyn
Rose
Stone

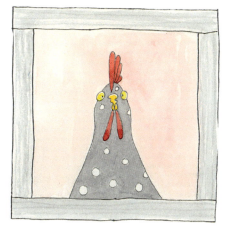

Red Robin Farm was like most farms. There was a barn and a silo. There was a tractor and a hay wagon. There were long grassy fields and rolling hills as far as the eye could see. And of course, there were animals—cows, pigs, ducks and sheep, a horse, a bull, a cat and a dog.

But what made Red Robin Farm unlike any other farm were four hens, named…

OLIVE   NAOMI   GERTRUDE   VERA

On most days, you could find them scratching in the dirt in the driveway, or pecking at bugs in the garden. On this day, however, they were bug-hunting in the tall grass near the barn.

And that's where all the commotion started.

Chapter One

Out of nowhere the hens heard two voices. One by one they poked their heads out of the grass and saw the farmer and his son walking toward them.

"We have no choice," the farmer said. "We've got to take the bull by the horns."

The moment the farmer and his son were out of sight, Olive turned to the others.

"Did you hear that?" she squawked.

"I most certainly did," Naomi replied.

"It's just dreadful," Gertrude muttered.

"This grass tickles," Vera giggled.

"Quick...everyone...follow me!" Olive shouted.

She marched around the corner of the barn and straight out to the pasture, where the cows were grazing near the fence. "Excuse me! We need to talk to you," she called out.

"Indeed we do," Naomi added.

"It's alarming," Gertrude warned.

"I love the view from here," Vera said.

The cows watched suspiciously as the hens ducked under the fence.

"Everyone remain calm," Olive told them, once they were all assembled.

The lead cow stopped chewing. "Is there a problem?"

"Yes," Olive replied. "The farmer is going to take the bull by the horns."

Naomi leaned forward and said, "We're not sure what's going to happen after that."

"But it sounds frightful," Gertrude clucked.

"We're lucky we don't have horns," Vera mumbled.

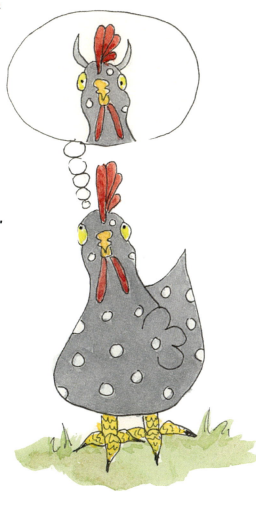

The lead cow began to chuckle. One by one, all the cows joined in. As their laughter grew louder, the hens looked back and forth at one another.

Was there something they missed?

Did someone say something funny?

There was nothing humorous about being grabbed by the head.

The lead cow stopped laughing and explained, "The barn roof leaks."

Another cow said, "The farmer keeps patching it, but each time he does, another leak starts somewhere else."

"Well, that's no reason for him to get mad at the bull," Olive snipped.

"It's not his fault the roof leaks," Naomi reasoned.

"I like the bull," Gertrude said. "He's very friendly."

"And so strong," Vera said with dreamy eyes.

"No, no, no," the lead cow said. "It's an expression. It means he's going to have to address a difficult situation. Maybe something he's been avoiding."

"He's probably going to have to replace the whole roof," another cow said.

"Have you seen the barn roof?" the lead cow asked. "It's huge."

"Well actually...no," Olive admitted.

"It's a little too high for my tastes," Naomi confessed.

"Much too shiny," Gertrude added.

"Hurts my eyes," Vera said, blinking at the cows.

"Well then," Olive said in a very official voice, "I'd say that settles that."

She turned away from the cows, raised her head high, and said to the others, "Come along, girls."

They walked back to the barn, then over to the flower bed along the front of the house to look for bugs.

Gertrude had just snapped up a tasty beetle when the still of the morning was broken by a loud SCREECH!

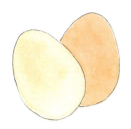

Chapter Two

Olive shouted, "Take cover!" and they all squeezed into a patch of purple-blue Iris plants.

"What is it?" Naomi whispered.

"Shush!" Gertrude said.

"Hey! No pushing," Vera groaned.

A large brown station wagon swerved wildly into the driveway and came to a grinding halt just ten feet away from where the hens were hiding. The dust was still settling when the driver's door opened and a woman from the Social Club stepped out.

"Oh, it's just her," Olive snipped.

"Blanche," Naomi sighed.

"Blanche who?" Gertrude asked.

"Gesundheit," Vera said.

The farmer's wife rushed out of the house to greet her and the two women immediately began whispering and giggling. Curious, the hens inched forward among the Irises, straining to hear the conversation.

"Why don't you come inside where it's nice and cool," the farmer's wife said in a louder voice. "I'll make us a nice pot of tea while you spill the beans."

"Well," Blanche giggled with a sly grin. "If you insist."

The two women hurried into the house, closing the door behind them.

Olive climbed out of the flowerbed and paced in a circle.

"This is bad," she said. "Very bad."

"It's unspeakable," Naomi said, following close behind her.

"What are they thinking?" Gertrude asked, joining in.

Vera shook her head back and forth. "Quit it! You're making me dizzy."

Olive stopped short and said, "We have to do something."

"Right away," Naomi insisted.

"What choice do we have?" Gertrude asked.

"I'm fresh out of ideas," Vera admitted.

"I know exactly what to do," Olive said. "Come with me."

They scampered across the yard and around the shed, to a large square pen where the pigs were sprawled out in the mud. Olive looked through the wire fencing and said, "Excuse me, may we have a word?"

The pigs snorted as they climbed to their feet. When they came close to the fence, the first pig looked at Olive and said, "Nice day, huh?"

"Well, yes, I suppose it is," Olive said, glancing up at the blue sky above.

The second pig said, "Come on in, the mud is perfect."

"No, thank you," Naomi said politely. "We prefer dry dirt."

Both pigs let out a snort.

"What do you know about beans?" Gertrude asked.

"You DO know what they are, don't you?" Vera said.

Both pigs snorted again.

"Of course we do," said the first pig.

"We're familiar with all foods," the second pig informed them.

"Well, something's about to happen at the farmer's house," Olive said.

"Something with beans," Naomi whispered.

"It's that crazy woman from the Social Club," Gertrude squawked.

"She's going to spill them," Vera said. "The beans, that is."

Both pigs started to laugh and snort. They laughed and snorted so hard that they fell into the mud and couldn't get up.

The four hens were very insulted.

After all, they were very strict about keeping things clean. Neatness was no laughing matter. Not that a pig would know anything about that.

The pigs finally stopped laughing and climbed to their feet. "The Social Club is having a pie contest," the first pig said.

"Well then, it's no time to have beans all over the floor," Olive pointed out.

"In the kitchen?" Naomi huffed. "Never."

"Someone could get hurt," Gertrude cried out.

"I think pies are delicious," Vera whispered to the first pig.

The second pig said, "She's not really going to spill any beans."

"It's an expression," the first pig explained. "It means she's going to tell the whole story. You know, every last detail about something."

"Like looking for bugs?" asked Olive.

"Or crickets?" Naomi chimed in.

"It could be earthworms," Gertrude said proudly.

"Or bubble gum," Vera suggested.

"No. I bet it's Dorothy Jensen's secret apple pie recipe," the second pig said.

"Yes! With Granny Smith apples," the first pig murmured.

"Uh huh," the second pig said. "And brown sugar and cinnamon."

"And oats," the first pig added.

"Ooh... oats!" the second pig grunted. "Yum!"

"Well, that settles that," Olive said in a stern voice, "Come along girls, we're leaving."

As they walked away, Vera said, "My cousin Penelope ate a bean once. It gave her the hiccups."

With that, the two pigs had heard enough. They went back to the middle of the pen and flopped down in the mud.

Olive, Naomi, Gertrude and Vera were halfway across the yard when a thunderous CLUNK! made them run to the lilac bushes for cover.

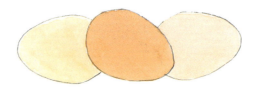

Chapter Three

Olive peeked out through the bushes and saw a rickety old box truck coming toward them. Its springs squeaked and groaned as it bounced down the driveway in a cloud of dust.

"False alarm," she shouted.

Naomi poked her head out. "Phew…that was close."

"You can say that again," Gertrude chimed in.

Vera closed her eyes and said, "Ahh…lilac…so relaxing."

They'd seen this truck before. It was the junk man. He was always stopping by to pick up this, or drop off that. The truck came to a stop near the house and the junk man honked the horn two times.

The farmer's wife stuck her head out the kitchen window. "Right over there," she called out, pointing across the yard. "The white elephants are in the shed."

Olive turned to the others. "Did you hear that? Tell me you heard that."

"Oh, I heard it alright," Naomi said, teetering nervously.

"I need to sit," Gertrude said, plopping herself down at once.

"What's this farm coming to?" Vera mumbled.

Olive stepped out of the bushes and began pacing back and forth, trying to decide what to do.

Then it came to her

"I've got it," she announced. "Follow me!"

She turned and hurried across the lawn, past the huge oak tree, to the lower field where a flock of sheep were grazing.

"We have some news!" she shouted as she ran towards them.

"You're not going to believe it," Naomi yelled.

"It's really big," Gertrude hollered.

"And heavy, too," Vera added.

The sheep, as a rule, were rather timid. When they saw the hens running toward them, shouting wildly, they moved closer together, forming a tight group. The four hens saw that and stopped running at once. They slowed to a walk and approached the sheep very slowly.

The largest sheep, standing in the front, stepped forward and said, "It might be better if you told me first. Wouldn't want to alarm the others."

They moved away from the flock, and when Olive spoke she kept her voice low. "There...are...elephants...nearby," she said.

"White elephants," Naomi whispered.

"They're in the shed," Gertrude revealed.

"How do they all fit in there?" Vera asked, looking back over her shoulder at the shed.

The largest sheep began to chuckle. When she went back and told the others what Olive had said, they all broke out in a fit of laughter. They laughed so hard that the little bells on their collars began to ring.

The hens were very insulted. Once again, they had no idea what was so funny.

Didn't the sheep realize what would happen if the elephants got out? They would trample everything in sight and make a horrible mess.

Before long, the whole farm would be in a panic.

When the sheep finally stopped laughing, the largest one came forward again. "The church is having a flea market this weekend," she said.

One of the other sheep said, "The farmer's wife asked the junkman to stop by and pick up a few things."

"Well, when he goes in the shed, he's going to get a BIG surprise," Olive told them.

"And he'll need a much bigger truck," Naomi said.

"Why would anyone want elephants at a flea market?" Gertrude asked.

"I hate fleas," Vera said. "They make me itch."

The largest sheep shook her head, trying to keep from laughing again. "They're not real elephants," she told the hens. "It's just an expression. A white elephant is another way to describe something that you don't want anymore. Something old, or useless."

"The shed's full of them," one of the other sheep yelled from the back row.

"You're sure of this?" Olive asked.

"Positive," the largest sheep replied.

"Well, in that case," Olive said, "we'll just be on our way."

She turned and marched across the lawn with Naomi, Gertrude and Vera following close behind. When they passed the shed, they heard loud noises coming from inside and quickly ran the other way.

Chapter Four

The four hens strolled past the barnyard and went into the hay field to look for crickets. That's where the farmer's son was picking up hay bales and throwing them onto a wagon, while the farmer stacked the load.

"That's it," the son said, as he threw on the last bale.

"And just in time," the farmer replied, looking up at the gathering clouds. "It's about to rain cats and dogs."

When the four hens heard that, they came to an immediate stop and began clucking loudly.

"TO THE HEN HOUSE!" Olive shouted.

Wasting no time at all, they ran as fast as they could toward the barn. On the way, they passed the horse, standing next to the fence.

Naomi screamed, "TAKE COVER!"

Gertrude was right behind her. "SAVE YOURSELF!"

Vera zigzagged back and forth. "I LOVE RUNNING!"

The horse was very confused.

As the hens ran past, he yelled, "WHOOOAAAAAAA."

The hens stopped running at once, knocking into one another in the process.

The horse asked, "What in the world is all this fuss about?"

"There's a terrible storm coming," Olive said in a nervous voice.

"And it's not rain," Naomi added.

"It's cats and dogs," Gertrude announced.

"How do they get up there?" Vera asked, looking up at the sky.

The horse broke out in a fit of laughter, pawing the ground with his front hoof.

Again, the hens were very insulted. Did he not see the clouds overhead? Maybe he didn't like cats and dogs. But that didn't make any sense. Who doesn't like cats and dogs? Either way, it was no reason to laugh.

When the horse finally calmed down, he said to the hens, "The farmer's got to get the hay into the barn before the storm comes."

"Well, actually," Olive said, "wouldn't it be better to leave it out?"

"Yes," Naomi said. "It would make a much softer place for the cats to land."

"And the dogs, too," Gertrude noted.

"I don't care much for hay," Vera whispered to the horse. "No flavor, and much too chewy."

The horse began to chuckle again. "Stop, stop," he said. "Cats and dogs are NOT going to fall out of the sky."

"How can you be so sure?" Olive asked him.

"'Raining cats and dogs' is an expression," he said. "It means that we're in for a really big downpour, maybe even thunder and lightning."

"No cats?" Naomi asked.

"No cats," the horse said.

"And no dogs?" Gertrude asked.

"No dogs," the horse said calmly.

Hearing that news, the hens began to relax.

Vera sniffed her feathers. "Actually, I could use a shower."

Olive stood up, straightened her feathers and said, "Well then, we best be getting back. We wouldn't want to be stuck out here in the rain." She turned and led the others through the field toward the barn.

Every few steps, Gertrude looked up, convinced that one of the dark clouds was following them. She tried to get the others to walk faster, but they were tired from all their running and were content to walk.

They crossed the yard and headed straight for the hen house where it was nice and dry. It had been a very hectic day, and once they were inside, they climbed up on their roosts and fell fast asleep.

They were so tired, they slept right through the rainstorm.

And the wild ruckus that followed.

Chapter Five

The farmer and his son were milking the cows in the barn when they got to talking, as they often did when they were working. Usually, the cows didn't pay much attention to them, but on this day, something the farmer said caught their attention right away. It was about the hired hand.

"It was the craziest thing you ever saw," the farmer said.

"I wish I could've been there," the son replied.

"Folks there said they'd never seen anything like it," the farmer exclaimed.

"Well, it's like they say," the son told him, "there's a first time for everything."

"I bet it makes the local news," the farmer declared.

"It's got to," the son said. "That boy's going to be famous now."

"Yup," the farmer said. "He really laid an egg."

They both began to laugh as the cows stood there in complete shock.

One of the cows whispered to another, "Is it true?"

The second cow shook her head. "It can't be true."

The first cow glared at her. "But they just said it."

"Well, then, I guess it must be so," the second cow said.

The situation demanded an immediate investigation. As soon as the milking was done, the cows got busy. When the farmer let them out into the barnyard, they walked over to the fence and called to the horse, who was standing in the pasture.

"We have some astounding news," the first cow said.

The horse trotted over at once. "Do tell," he whinnied.

"Uh, it's a little weird," another cow warned.

The first cow leaned forward and said, "The hired hand laid an egg."

"Whaaaat?" the horse replied.

"It's true," the first cow said. "We heard it straight from the farmer's own mouth, not ten minutes ago."

"That's right," the second cow confirmed. "He said it was the strangest thing he'd ever seen."

"That's unbelievable," said the horse.

"Tell me about it," the first cow replied, shaking her head. "Do us a favor. See what you can find out."

"Sure thing," the horse told them. "I know just where to start."

He turned and galloped across the pasture to the duck pond. Ducks knew about eggs, he figured. They were sure to have some information.

But when the ducks heard the news, they began quacking loudly and waddling about in a wild frenzy.

It was an outrage.

Why hadn't they been consulted?

What kind of egg was it?

Who was taking care of it?

What did it look like?

After the horse left, they flew over to the orchard to talk to the sheep. The sheep had good ears, so it was a safe bet that they'd heard something about the egg. But when the ducks explained the situation, the sheep didn't know what to think.

"The hired hand?" said one.

"He laid an egg?" asked another.

It was all very curious. After a lengthy discussion, they decided to go see the pigs. Everyone knew that pigs were good at sniffing things out. If anyone would know the facts, it was sure to be them.

But when the pigs heard about the hired hand, they became very angry. They began to snort and squeal. After all, he was their friend. He was the one that always fed them. Why didn't he tell them he was going to lay an egg? They felt completely betrayed.

Sensing there was more to the story than the sheep were telling them, the pigs decided to ask the dog. Who better to dig up the facts of the story than the dog? He was always digging up something. Surely he would know about the hired hand's now-famous egg.

When the dog heard that the pigs were looking for him, he came running as fast as he could. When he got to the pigpen, the pigs were waiting for him.

"Sit," they told him.

"Excuse me?" he said.

"No, really. It's better if you sit," they explained.

This must be big news, he thought to himself, as he sat down on

the grass.

"Have you heard about the egg?" the first pig asked.

"Well, let's see," the dog said, thinking. "I think it came first...or was it the chicken? I'm not really sure."

"No, no, no," grunted the other pig. "Not that egg."

"We're talking about the hired hand," said the first pig.

"He laid an egg," the second pig explained.

The dog leaned closer. "Say again?"

"The hired hand laid an egg," they both said at the same time.

The dog began to laugh. "You're pulling my leg," he said.

"Nope," the first pig said. "The farmer said so himself."

"Might even make the news," the second pig squealed.

The dog looked at each of them suspiciously. This sounded like another pig joke. After a few minutes, he still wasn't convinced. It was simply too strange to believe.

The truth was, no one knew what to believe, and by the time the story had made the rounds, the whole farm was in a panic. Finally, the cows decided it was time to gather all the animals together and calm them down. This egg business had gotten way out of hand and someone had to put a stop to it. So, just after dinner, they assembled at the corner of the barnyard to settle the matter once and for all.

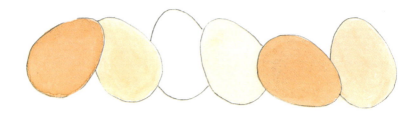

Chapter Six

Olive, Naomi, Gertrude and Vera yawned and stretched their wings as they woke up from their long and restful nap.

"Well, I feel much better," Olive said.

"Yes," Naomi murmured. "That was just what I needed."

"Nothing like an afternoon nap," Gertrude said in a chipper voice.

"I was dreaming about elephants eating beans," Vera confessed.

"Elephants DO NOT eat beans," Gertrude maintained.

"Are you sure?" asked Naomi.

"How would they?" asked Gertrude.

"With hot dogs, of course," said Vera.

Because they'd been napping in their hen house, none of them knew about the meeting. Of course, they hadn't heard about the hired hand and his egg, either.

When they came walking down the ramp of the hen house, however, they couldn't help but notice the gathering at the corner of

the barnyard.

"I wonder what that's all about?" Olive asked.

"It looks like a meeting," Naomi suggested.

"Or a party," Gertrude added.

"I love parties," Vera said. "Maybe they'll have cake."

As they approached the barn, they saw the cows standing at

the far end of the barnyard. On the opposite side of the fence, in the pasture, were the horse and the bull and the sheep. To the right of the barnyard were the pigs, sticking their heads through the pigpen gate.

Meanwhile, sitting on the lawn and talking among themselves were the ducks. Right behind them, the cat and the dog sat waiting for things to get underway.

When Olive, Naomi, Gertrude and Vera came walking up, all the animals turned at once and looked at them. That's when they realized that no one had told the hens about the hired hand, or the farm's newest egg. Suddenly it grew very quiet.

"Good evening to all," Olive said in a pleasant voice.

"Lovely night for a get-together," Naomi noted.

"We really should do this more often," Gertrude said.

"Do you see any cake?" Vera whispered, looking around.

They were just about to sit down on the grass when the lead cow spoke up.

"We have something to tell you," she said.

"Something very strange," the horse muttered.

"Quite frankly," quacked one of the ducks, "we think the whole situation was handled in a very unprofessional manner."

"Indeed," another duck agreed. "So insulting."

The pigs agreed and began to snort loudly.

"What seems to be the problem?" Olive asked.

"I'm not sure how to tell you this," the lead cow said slowly.

"Go ahead, tell them," the other cows called out in unison.

"Yes, tell them!" shouted the cat and the dog.

The lead cow looked at the hens and said, "It's about the hired hand."

Here it comes, thought the sheep, who bunched together in a tight group.

"Uh-oh," the pigs snorted, backing away from the gate.

"Get ready to run," the bull whispered to the horse.

The ducks, true to their name, ducked down, and the cat slinked behind the dog.

"The hired hand?" Olive asked. "What about him?"

The lead cow hesitated briefly, then said, "He laid an egg."

There was a moment of total silence as the animals waited for the hens to react.

Olive responded first. She broke the silence with a single laugh. Then Naomi started to chuckle. Gertrude let out a snicker and Vera began to giggle. Before long, the four of them were laughing so hard that they fell on the ground, kicking their tiny hen feet in the air.

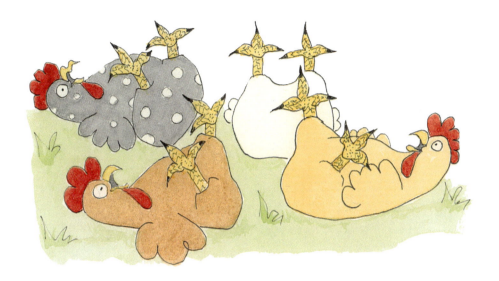

While this was going on, the other animals watched in disbelief.

"What's so funny about an egg?" one of the ducks quacked.

"How rude," the largest sheep blatted.

The pigs began to snort.

The cows didn't know what to think. They certainly hadn't planned on this type of reaction.

It took a few minutes, but when the hens finally stopped laughing, Olive said, "The hired hand went to the county fair with his sweetheart."

"That is NOT an appropriate place to lay an egg," one of the ducks shouted.

"It's unsanitary!" quacked another.

That got the hens laughing all over again.

As their laughter died down, Naomi said, "He wanted to impress her, so he entered the pie eating contest."

"Well of course he did," one of the sheep said. "He must have been very hungry after laying the egg."

The hens laughed even harder. When they caught their breath, Gertrude explained, "He set an all-time record for pie eating."

When the pigs heard that, they squealed with glee.

"But he made a terrible mess," Vera said. "He got pie everywhere."

"Did he get any on the egg?" the dog asked.

"Yes, yes, what about the EGG?" the horse demanded.

Olive shook her head. "There was no egg," she said loudly.

"I think you're mistaken," one of the cows replied.

"Yes, I'm afraid so," said another. "We heard the farmer quite clearly. He said it was the hired hand."

"And it was definitely an egg," a third cow added.

"It's an expression," Naomi told them.

"It means to fail at something," Gertrude said.

"I prefer the word 'flop,'" Vera whispered to the nearest sheep.

Hearing this, the animals were even more confused. As they stood there trying to sort it out, Olive said, "The farmer thinks the hired hand failed to impress his sweetheart."

"Because he made such a pig of himself with the pies," Naomi explained. She looked over at the pigs and whispered, "Sorry about that."

But the pigs didn't mind. They'd heard it before. Besides, they were proud of the hired hand. He had eaten like a champ.

That's when Gertrude let them in on a little secret. "The farmer was wrong," she told them.

"That's right," Vera said. "The sweetheart was actually very impressed."

The animals looked confused again, so the hens spelled it out for them.

"She loves to cook," Olive said.

"He loves to eat," Naomi explained.

"They left the fair together…" Gertrude began.

"Wait! I want to tell, I want to tell," Vera interrupted.

"OK, fine… you tell them," Gertrude sighed.

"They got married the very next day," Vera swooned.

With that, the animals let out a huge cheer that echoed all the way down to the lower pasture.

With the mystery of the egg finally solved, Olive, Naomi, Gertrude and Vera went back across the yard to look for crickets in the tall grass next to the shed.

"Can you believe that?" Olive said to the others.

"The hired hand, laying an egg," Naomi chuckled.

"That really takes the cake," Gertrude said.

"THERE WAS CAKE?" Vera cried out.

The other three hens turned to Vera and yelled,
"It's an expression!"

OLIVE
(New Hampshire Red)
New Hampshire Reds are medium-sized, family-friendly birds that are easy to tame and make great pets. Curious, trusting and personable, they are happy to forage in the yard looking for tasty treats and will lay approximately 200 eggs per year.

NAOMI
(Buff Orpington)
Buff Orpingtons are docile and friendly. Their demeanor is calm and stately, but they can run quickly, particularly if food is involved. They love attention and even like being cuddled. They will lay between 200 and 280 eggs per year.

GERTRUDE
(White Leghorn)
White Leghorns have a lovely temperament, but are not fond of being touched. Inquisitive and independent, they can be difficult to tame. Extremely prolific egg layers, they can produce 280 to 320 medium sized white eggs per year.

VERA
(Barred Rock)
Mellow birds, Barred Rocks are beautiful, calm and productive. Very adaptable, they get along well with birds and humans alike. Named for the grayish rock pattern of their feathers, they are inquisitive and love to forage for food. A Barred Rock will lay 200 to 280 brownish-pink eggs per year.

About the Author
Alfred M. Struthers (alfredstruthers.com) lives in Peterborough, New Hampshire, with his wife and their incorrigible dog, Manny. When he isn't crafting books that inspire, entertain, and make a difference in the lives of young readers, Mr. Struthers is a singer/songwriter, a furniture maker, and an avid collector of the fossils that line the stream beds around Cooperstown, New York.
In addition to *Did You Hear That?*, he has published four books in his popular Third Floor Mystery Series: *The Case of Secrets, The Phantom Vale, The Curse of Halim,* and *The Demon Tide*.

About the Illustrator
Cathy Provoda lives in Peterborough, New Hampshire, with her partner Richard and their cat, Diesel. When not painting, she can be found in her gardens or playing bluegrass music on her autoharp. Years ago while raising her two sons, Ms. Provoda shared a small farm with a cow named Daisy, four goats, rabbits, and a flock of chickens. Today, the chickens raised by her oldest grandson are the inspiration for her whimsical and comical chicken characters. She is the founder of Blueberry Cove Creations (blueberrycovecreations.com), where she sells wildlife note cards and chicken-centric greeting cards. *Did You Hear That?* is her first book.

Made in the USA
San Bernardino, CA
28 January 2020